david brazil

PLATE XIX

OXFORD, CORPUS CHRISTI COLLEGE, MS. 255A, FOL. 12*v*.

THE *Arbores* OF JOACHIM OF FIORE (pp. 124–36)

The events of them like images on a shield,
we carry thru the streets of the town.

aevum

we're that preterite where
what appears
that has this fate:
to come within
the strand of light
    where we, half dead & living still
continue every prior folded in like
echoes, orphans

                of phenomena
ate of aevum & now (sempiternal)
cant step off,

the obligation's binding & we're
        bound,   to wear our
            faces, to have
                    worn.

the halo's idesthai
this donates
a pure potential

wove with
works of earth's
affectus

to which add
this **what we gloss as**
grace, a term dug
out from   grave of
saints and graves of
martyrs, them were
witnesses.

an anvelope
betwixt   the qualia
                quantifies such

ache or wound in
time we are,
poured forth from hule's
hole, an accent on
this   accident befalling
form, a fickle flex that's
folded into mneme's

heptaplus, which you back
into when you're backing up to see the
zip

a **species** rose,
   unfolded almost of
     thy law,   in
  dishonor raised
  in doxa,

     having done the
      pirouette,
the trace or shadow of
   some sign says
    physis, still
in echo from the
     civic stone

    beneath the Market, --
yesterday if was,
   today who knows.

a certain hollow
veiled with shadow
under song whose
notes are points delimiting
a zone of recall, where
love was & where love's
wasted,

              whence
this vertical **else**
discalced & singular should
rise before such him as
ah art 'ou –

who shall scape whipping
in scathe of appear

57. Die Königin von Saba besucht Salomon. Paradiestür
Florenz, Baptisterium

gild-songs

set the world on six and sevene

000.

monuments our moments lashed
to daily tempests fast and thick
that beat the brainstem damn near mashed
by heap we weep up brick by brick

and our world altar red with blood
such as was spattered since the flood
where we with sinful reason cry
if it's an abbatoir then why

000.

we took an oath in time itself
and frequented its law
who Sinai's hem left on the shelf
to pick and choose and haw

o Mitras is a modicum
of mercy in your veil
to plait a florilegium
of pacts we pledge and fail

for freedom's just another word
for being corporate sin
which echoes through the age unheard
by us who dwell within

so make a promise make a pact
to bind yourself to time
within whose womb's the counterfact
which reads the reckoned rime

and make a promise make a pact
and tie it in your mind
and time will come wherein that fact
will be an awesome find

000.

My lover Law I lay the neume
upon our sing to make our room
that time may flourish as it must
and leave us lovings that wont rust

for what a flower of this State
should come in time to designate
would leave me sick of such constraint
as shall be sung in this complaint

or given lay of time's gray edge
where we are stranded in the sedge
and bracken of the thoroughfare
and sorted into what wont care

and what can carry through the days
all florid splendors of the praise
we lay upon the right we saw
to sing us up in to the law

000.serpent song

offspring shat out on this strand
to lick the law and chant the band
come follow my most subtle art
to salt the rite & fuck the heart

000.

Lady lave the widow's
bones in pollen
blood of *intellectus*
sol or else a

house you built from
            inner Sun,
                    to

torque by inches so the
hidden's known, and

how hard heart to split from
what blood wants, our

bowls & tendrils,
grasses of this earth.

000.

them's our flags
cash o'er walls
and fearful as
a figured ground
on which we tread,
our cancelled crypt,
as amble we
across raw strand

for books our kings
so stand from grunt,
that each one's eye may light

000.chant of those in impure office

At your wall we wreak the filth
and pluck the lilacs from their beds
we kill the ones who must be killed
and fluff the pillows neath your heads

your city makes us multitudes
cast just beyond its seas of glass
behold our frozen attitudes
and hear our cry *Alas Alas*

your architecture of the ring
wont run without we scoria
who antipodal to the king
still sing our gutter Gloria

& all your vowels we shall shed
until at last we lie down dead
in loss of this our human face
while others come to take our place

and every day we feel the chill
of resignation to the will
of Him we nominate Most High
who speaks we live or speaks we die

So let this pennant bear the mark
of all us left outside the ark
who shant on dry shore disembark
but gather in the growing dark

000.

pure ether pours
through this remember
as a cranny in the
really

to lay milk &
gladiolus, our aromas
of the *aevum*

so to furnish
our liturgics we
come human fleshing
fountains

that we may appoint aright
our undying cellular body of light

000.

Early eve, light lamp, suck
water, shit & work, go
pluck a brick from
villaged yip of
keening plea today, o
drink it up to skip pitched portals breaker
ram like
skinned and broiled
fruits whole
village from despoliation seeking
fucking method.
Scan 'er.
Gloss it in the
west, set words, a
million fucking bricks fell out, and
how's it other than when
you were live and how'd it
get back tonic building *to-*
nos in a line to learn your deeper
love for matter.   Prick the
plain and
pluck the fucking picking, others make an
other thing with brick, so
wall the valley kid or else you
seek a stamp butt end it ciphers
Semiramis if I reckon right

000.in may

We so mad when we be merry
sucking off our nature's cherry
pirating the sordid earth
for all such seeds as may be worth

a ducat in the destitution
of our home land's dissolution
lacking luster whose ablution
water's nature's prostitution

so say salt and cast it out
and sing our chant and wring our shout
so Ballers what ye all about
& may we trust or shall we doubt

upon this festive first of May
for outside freedom starts today
though it's a solitary way
for we who work & pay & pay

with singing spirits destitute
but let me tune my fucking lute
and pluck ye up your urban flute
so we may hymn our absolute

000.song of type

Judges silent on our hearts
turn up the tomb of worldly parts
that add up to our heap of hours
pontifexes of the flowers

judges show us silent sign
to indicate that they divine
which one shall be our hallowed hell
to wallow in that asphodel

so shall my light afford the edge
of what each judge will there allege
may it transpire for each wrong
I render up this single song:

Song of flower that has flowed,
song of unitary node,
song of type and song of sign,
and song of what on earth was mine

I folded in this little book
I fished out with a fleshy hook

000.giants

Those tumuli so
pale upon the sea?   O,
giants.   Tons of ways to
get to shore, our
country's bare & bleeds its most
to tickle its autochthonical kids,
and where was your zone of arrest.
You listed into scenes of
unthreshed loves, projected
native lands, it's
here, it pours out through this
octaved reed, let's get specific.   Rest
your feed and gloss your bio, giants
don't come cheap.   They
ordered forts our
waves still slap, impatient for the end of
epic.   Dad ground glyphs into the reaches of our
island's magic table, early on, no
shame to be a pirate, you'd just ask:
Are you a pirate?   Keep your
kid, give wind a shelter.
Sovereignty's a spring so
bear in mind the
song is past.   We're gonna need a
house if it's to happen, spirit needs a
house.   When pyre's gone white ash and
char you dump the wine on chunks of
bone that still remain, and
that's the rite.   So heed the humid
steam that hisses, billows will always now
cling to your clothes.

000.our song

Our figured fate
has flowered out
down by the gate
where pent we shout

so vowels sluice
into the song
expelling juice
of what went wrong

when we now gone
and yet outlawed
sprawled out upon
the knee of God

where lay we dumb
with naught to say
till Shiloh come
to show the way

the way that's fashioned
from our bones
and our impassioned
mobile phones

000.ring shout for augurs

As oracles we always say
whatever fates the daughters may
decree in this our age of law
whose single flesh is all you saw

and how this word came to our nation
making flesh for revelation
so we might enjoy salvation
is our only conversation

thus we pace the city's ring
and alternately weep and sing
and have no option but to bring
our news that doesnt mean a thing

for we proclaim what is is not
is only spirit just now caught
inside a scrap with which it fights
for all its sempiternal rights

the flesh of which is all you saw
within your former age of law
which fate might even name today
so always must we augurs say

islets

...each grassy oe...

if freer
        by will
   Gottes zeichen my   occident <u>nakba</u> attuned by
      poles to they garment knit from leaves of
         This the tree of death, primeval
   face in
       missa media waters of
              lay trembling amidst song

so graceful given there my Daughters to
       your restless Paramours,

so let the holy city lift its skirt, attend,

      prócessing o prócessing▦ as a
            circuit of the sun

     who owns this world & you by fate and fire,
                fate and fire,

     symptoms of your holy love,
        convi[n]c[c]ted of your dirt, &
 let to part, my Adam's son, my
             o
       cherished ▦ most
     o you're
cherished ^ borne up by your hair

~~die Wende dem Zeiten by~~   to<u>cc</u>ata no<u>r</u>ma
                    ~~prophecy~~   turn of times by
        ~~toccata norma~~   prophecy by
                    ~~by~~ river ~~of~~ Chebar, by the
            bay of being where I had my second
                                                    within
                ~~cup of~~ coffee, set this down, still point ▦ ~~the~~ a
mount ~~mountain of the Law, so~~   of bring Law so
            send ~~sent~~ a signal PASS a
        signal PASS abet the remnant, still to they who
                        yeast amidst this ransack every
            idol of the heart, ~~clarifying~~ who clarify ~~the~~ a
                        templum there as thing to cut, as they to cut,
                                    of
        in ~~the~~ wilderness ~~the~~ word &
                    noplace else
    an oath alone could be the seed of all these fractious tribes
                could but men stand
                                in
        could ~~but they~~ stand ~~un~~oscillant within recess of
                they but
                                grace
        according to the Shadow he has built it, Bezalel,
                with knowledge & wi[y]th wisdom & in
            spirit gone before hum like a
                cloud the only road ~~we therefore~~ therefore we
                        save the broken tables also
                    save the broken tables

my soul among the lion so it
    climb the tree of nation to a
    field of holy apples where she dwelt &
      where she dwelt,

and   tell me Daughters of the prosper tell
        me Signals of the righteous well undo
            my flesh so that it ~~better sing your law,~~
                  sing now how it felt,

as ~~so~~ high notes of the battlefield or
      birth into this wildness sustained by
      nursing father feeds us
          milk out of his tit

an emblem that returned us yet
      to fates as the bare postulants at
      reversed rooting supplicating
      sucking ~~stones for days~~ on the shit

but prophecy Arise ~~in us~~ and sing
      ~~all borne out from the grips that held~~
      from all of what   the day shall bring
and let us pass the devil ring
    and let us see the heart of Things
    and see that we may serve the King

but prophecy Arise and sing
      from ▓▓▓ ▓▓▓ ▓▓▓ the day shall bring
        all of what
    that we may pass the devil ring
      ~~and see that we may serve the king~~
      and seeing souls may serve the king

my soul among the lion so it
climb the tree of nation to a
field of holy apples where she dwelt &
where she dwelt,

and tell me Daughters of the prosper tell
me Signals of the righteous well undo
my flesh so that it
sing now how it felt,

as high notes of the battlefield or
birth into this wilderness sustained by
nursing father feeds us
milk out of his tit

an emblem that returned us yet
to fates as the bare postulants at
reversed rooting supplicating
sucking on the shit

but prophecy Arise and sing
from all of what the day shall bring
that we may pass the devil ring
and seeing souls may serve the King

~~feel~~ left to feel

my age,
      my debts,
            ~~my rhythms,~~
my rhythms ~~in rhythm just as~~ salved from
      face where all communion gathers, face

of world or
        ^{or}
    face of light,^kairos as the
   ^{times}
time gives way be{'}neath ~~the~~ pressure{s} of the ~~gathered~~ ice
              _____

so Ithaca, so ~~it~~
          ~~gathers up in~~ bodies only
   semblance of the accidence ~~toward light~~ or
            fate of ~~a~~ man or
     fate of one just house or
             ^{of}
      this blue sky on ~~my~~ given day ~~of~~ yours or
              _____

   ^{o still}   ^{and}   ^a
opus^~~yet~~ most infinite~~ly grand~~ small still
         _{vast's}

~~the stone that the builders rejected~~

~~small still stone~~ the builders ~~rejected still reject~~
small ~~mute~~ mineral   who are building still reject

One of many
measures given ▓ providence in
origin, so he is born
the ~~on~~ very day when wickedness{,} ~~achieves its apex, worldly, so~~
when wickedness

---

rune
& strewn amidst the ~~ruin~~ of ~~an education in the~~ rite we
an education   could partake, ~~lost son,~~ who's   figured
plural
son   ~~figured~~ throughout ^ fields ~~all~~ ~~crying father father~~   o
lamenting
~~father~~
providence   o   ~~father father father~~ providence

---

hearts are
and   were it time it would be time when ~~we are~~ gathered ~~in our~~
as unities as sureties   as
histories   ~~hearts to history as unity in~~ terror{s} of the Name,
▓▓▓▓▓▓▓▓ ▓▓

so utter this my fathomless

~~when you go gathering~~

~~white artemisia~~

my fathomless gone gathering
gone gathering gone gathering
when ▓ ▓ white artemisia ▓ came

One of many measures given
providence in origin,
so he is born the very day
when wickedness, when wickedness

and strewn amidst the rune of rite
an education could partake
who's figured son through plural fields
o providence, o providence

and were it time it would be time
when gathered hearts are histories
as unities as sureties
as terrors of the Name

so utter this my fatherless
my fathomless gone gathering
gone gathering gone gathering
what white artemisia came

A rid
stretch, the
            pay, the
                    fee, for
vestige ~~or a~~ body ~~a~~ or a
        middle ~~medieval~~ body (plen-
stuffed with ~~itude of~~ <u>fate</u>), and
                    ▓ reconciled ~~o~~
    in this pardon in a
                    diptych so
conciliar, toward which we
are riding desert nurselings of
the law;
                ~~for spirit came~~   to rupture
    syntax cometh spirit
~~syntax~~   ~~to rupture syntax, it was said but~~   said it was but
        now ~~I now~~ {I} say, so
    read the scroll of age another way & angel ~~it the~~ up the
▓   ~~angel it in prison with your~~ scroll ~~of age in prison with your fraction~~
        ~~fraction of the song~~   of the song

    scroll of age when you in
        prison with your fraction of the
                        song

When hinging Spirit act as
            picture saving portion in the
      pivot, ask ~~an~~ your age an'
         will   ~~age if~~ it ~~would~~ murmur in the
                  ░░░░░░░ woods for ~~elements of~~   elementals
                              ~~heritance for~~
we have rendered ~~here~~ up~~on~~ this shore such works as would
            be bridges ~~to your~~
                        ~~palisdae~~ of Union, when
      the worlds may answer to themselves in ~~judgment of the~~   judge of
                  antiphon, for when ~~I saw my~~   at distance
saw my body ~~at such distance~~ on the earth atop the ~~apex of a~~   verdict
                  ~~pyre of the verdict say~~   say
      What woman have ░ we done within the square of worldly houses ░

            rescued
            ~~brought~~ we ~~up~~ the eye of soul from all this carnal policy?

      A chapter of the civic rolls on by,
         we serve the bread,
               we look to union where the heaven just meant sky. All
                  these little figures you cant read.

      And civic chapters roll on by
      And we ░░░░░░ serve ~~the~~ bread our family made
      And ~~we~~ look to union in the sky of
            little figures yall cant read.

but soul is
~~is~~ poor

not fed ~~from~~
~~day~~ from day

~~the naked word~~   ~~beneath the moon~~   beneath the ~~word~~ wound
~~beneath the moon~~   ~~the naked word~~   the naked ~~wound~~ word

lest they
should turn

their voice
unheard

and day &
night

~~the light of~~   our houses
~~houses~~   light

but soul is
poor

not fed
from day

beneath the
wound

the naked
word

lest they should
turn

their voice
unheard

and day &
night

our houses
light

            gimme gimme
                        lineament
(1.   that I might rise
                        ~~in~~ to ~~his~~ equities

        for Knights & riders
(2.   follow ~~like the~~ Fates ~~on horseback,~~
                                ~~shaveless after endless days of~~

            ~~roving~~ in ~~the~~ Open war
                up to the Gates

                                                        intercut
                    so signal Page ~~to~~ ~~move our precinct~~
        ~~intercut with holograms of angels out of Asia~~
        all   all   when   ~~in Spirit's bleakness~~   Spirit's bleak
        ~~all~~ ^ left ^ bereft ~~from failure of the Spirit to sublate itself it~~
        and moving ~~into~~ in the interdict   ~~moves within the interstices~~
                ~~Making Perfect Weakness~~   to pérfect ~~by such~~ strength we weak

                        * * *

        ~~For well you know~~   so signal Page to intercut
        ~~if you wont have~~   of   speak
            ~~the bitter Christ then~~   all left bereft ~~by~~ Spirit's ~~bleak~~
        ~~you s~~   and moving in the interdict
                                         ~~perfect by strength tho we gone weak~~
                                         ~~make perfect~~   ~~we gone weak~~
                                         shape perfect strength for we gone weak

        (4.   For you will have
              the bitter Christ or   and
              perish eating [h]Honey   (3.   ~~so~~ signal Page to interrupt
                                              all left bereft of Spirit speak
                                        and ~~then~~ and mobile in the interval
                                              shape perfect strength for we gone
                                                                        weak.

        (5.   and in that yonder
              Countrey there you'll
              never want for Money

Gimme gimme
lineament
that I might rise
to Equities

for Knights & riders
follow Fates
in Open war
up to the Gates

and signal Page to interrupt
all left bereft of Spirit speak
and mobile in the interval
shape perfect strength for we gone weak

for you will have
the bitter Christ or
perish eating Honey

and in that younger
Countrey there you'll
never want for Money

revelation's ~~education~~ tutor taxes
        while old pal the waste it waxes
   record heat   Septentrion
       a thousand channels   nothing on

     o most calm & most serene
     city built on gasoline
  our mother nature has a cancer
               her
      open wide & let ~~it~~ answer

I am ~~just a~~ predicate,
        ~~aa~~ predicate,
             a predicate,
  I am ~~just~~ a predicate
    whose subject is someplace out there.

♪

     Banners flap in the sultry breeze,
        home
   ~~and my old land got bad disease~~   and where I'm from got bad disease
                   and
   ~~and doctor says that there's no cure~~ ^ sawbones says there is no cure
   ~~for famine sickness death & war~~
   for sickness famine death & war

      us   us
  Give ~~me~~ meter give ~~me~~ rhyme
     we   a
    and ~~I~~ will make from flesh a ~~time~~ ~~such~~ time
to   ~~that~~ pours into this desert place
               all our
    and ~~to~~ nourish ~~up~~ ~~my~~ desperate race

  and then there's no pasture no pasture no pasture
  ~~d~~ so go out and ~~has~~ ask her and ask her and ask her
  and who was it ~~fa~~ fought her and fought her and fought her
  who lives without water no water no water

♪

  on busted plain a thinking reed / with grace & grace & grace indeed

Revelation's tutor taxes
while old pal the waste it waxes
record heat   Septentrion
a thousand channels   nothing on

o most calm & most serene
city built on gasoline
our mother Nature has a cancer
open wide & let her answer

Banners flap in sultry breeze,
and where I'm from got bad disease
and sawbones sez there is no cure
for sickness famine death & war

Give us meter give us rhyme
and we will make from flesh a time
to pour into this desert place
and nourish all our desperate race

and then there's no pasture no pasture no pasture
so go out and ask her and ask her and ask her
and who was it fought her & fought her & fought her
who lives without water no water no water

on busted plain a thinking reed / with grace & grace & grace indeed (schema) born to

me ████████ as

mudra (of a

cosmos)│ ~next to~ ████████ water, land & shelter gather

████ cloth of human labor where ████████ ████████ █

████████ most potent/ ~stories flower~ ████████ ████ ████

~from the~ shadow ████████████

foremost curse ⚫ upon the ████████ ~parcel,~

████ ████ ████ ████ ████ • ████ •• ████

history you divvy up ██ █ ████ ████

████████ ████ ████ you ██ hid your vices ██ o ~my~

████████ preacher ⚫

tell me cloud or tell me sky or

tell me ████ ~whose is~

mystery, for ████ ~what have~ ^they ████

forsaken me, so ███ in ~^A~ ████ town • ~or~ ████ ~further~ on |

████ my name is what it lack the

root a

moon came over hills last ████████████ ~night the~

~wife ; |~ beheld it all the

neighbors spilled in to the street to say that they had seen the

blood when dragons ate the only ~kid~ ████ fought in ~the~

law for spark of soul in us the one who would not

~bow~ ████████ among us in our native place ~that~ ████ bitter o most bitter o

the enemy of man

(schema) born to

me ~~invisible~~ as

mudra (of a

next to
cosmos)~~,~~ ~~just alongside~~ water, land & shelter gather

~~to a~~ cloth of human labor where ~~we err in~~   ~~erred in~~

stories flower
~~naming that~~ most potent / ~~story floweth from the~~

from the   shadow~~, flowereth, in~~

foremost curse ~~a~~ upon the ~~earth of~~ parcel,

~~utterance to nail you there, to parcels of a~~

history you divv[u]y up ~~like spoils after~~

~~cards called cleaner~~ you ~~have~~ hid your vices ~~my~~   o my

~~itinerant~~ preacher~~,~~

tell me cloud or tell me sky or

tell me ~~what is~~   whose is

what have
mystery, for ~~which~~ ^ they ~~have~~

a   or   further
fors[k]a[a]ken me, so ~~that~~ in ~~another~~ town a ~~little~~ ~~further~~ on &

~~west~~ my name is what it lack the

root a
moon came over hills last ~~evening wife & I~~ night the

wife & I   beheld it all the

neighbors spilled in to the street to say that they had seen the

kid
blood when dragons ate the only ~~child~~ fought in the

law for spark of soul in us the one who would not

that
bow   ~~supplicate~~ among us in our native place ~~the~~ bitter o most bitter o

the enemy of man

love   ~~love~~ can come among the living ~~living~~

incense, bread and ministration,

so ~~we~~ sat at ~~n knees~~ of gods at   *(sat we · needs)*

needful ~~f~~ portals waiting for to fetch ~~it, and~~ it,

_____

fr[l]olicked ~~there in lonesome~~ rental markets ~~going~~ rockets going   *(in our)*

~~up and fucking~~ up like hope, like

say ~~that it was you and me down there among the~~ ~~we are the~~ that   *(that it's just us · that)*

we are / ~~we're the~~   kids of man, and Satan rampant like a cancer ~~looking who~~ seeking

who

may he devour, all my streets become a province I

become the way, ^ white are ~~the~~ birds that come   *(so)*

to   chatter ~~their~~ Latin, so ~~the crows go~~ Sara ~~crows go~~ ^ Sundays   *(~~and then~~ · ~~then on~~)*

crows go   crazy, ~~on a Sunday morning, Sara,~~ ~~I am glad that~~   *(~~crazy~~ · I'm)*

so glad that   you are strong let's lift ~~up~~ prayers ~~for up~~ for   *(up)*

Valerie   ~~pray for Valerie~~ & ~~pray~~ Lord ~~for~~ the sick & those who   *(~~prayer~~ · o)*

have not where to sleep against the fatal

cold, o Lord, the mists of this damned year,

wherein they took the cudgel, Lord, so may a

calender unfold so fas & nefas taking

turns like twins with malediction, o my

love it knows no end, ~~and~~ for I have heard the

~~I have heard the~~ silence of the people.

love can come among the living
incense, bread and ministration,
so sat we ~~at~~ at needs of gods at
needful portals waiting for to fetch it,

———————

~~frolicked~~
frolicked in our rental markets rockets going
up like hope like
sat that <u>we</u> are
kids of man and Satan rampant like a cancer seeking who
     ^{he}
may ~~be~~ devoured ~~so the~~
so the streets became a province I became a way

———————

     ^{then}   ^{the}
~~and~~ ^ so white the ~~birds that come to~~ Latin clouds on
                       ^{on}
~~chatter~~ ▒▒▒ ~~Latin, so Sara~~ Sundays ~~the crows go~~ Sara crows go
~~crows~~ ▒▒ ~~go~~ crazy, I'm so
glad that you are strong ~~let's lift up prayers for and~~ so
——————— ~~so~~ let's lift up a prayer;

for   Valerie o Lord the sick & those who
have not where to sleep / against the fatal
cold, o Lord, the mists of this damned year,
~~wh~~
wherein they took the cudgel, Lord, so may a
calendar unfold so f<u>as</u> & n<u>e</u>fas taking
turns like twins with maledictions o my

———————

     ^{can}   ^{o Lord for}
love ~~it~~ knows no ~~end,~~ ~~for~~ I have heard the
silence of the people.

love can come among the living
incense, bread and ministration,
so sat we at needs of gods at
needful portals waiting for to fetch it,

———————————

frolicked in our rental markets rockets going
up like hope like
say that we are
                          rampant Satan seeking like a
kids of man and ~~Satan rampant like a cancer seeking who~~
~~he may devour~~   ~~may he devour~~   cancer to devour

———————————

so the streets bec[o]ame a province I bec[o]ame a way

———————————

and   then so white the Latin clouds on
Sunday Sara crows go
crazy I'm so
glad that you are strong so
              let's lift up a prayer;

———————————

for Valerie o Lord the sick & those who have
not where to sleep ~~against the fatal~~
~~cold o Lord the~~   against the fatal cold o Lord the
~~mists of this damned year,~~   mist of our made year,

———————————

wherein they took the cudgel, Lord, so may a
calendar unfold so fas & nefas taking
turns like twins with maledictions o my

———————

love can know no end o Lord for
I have heard the silence of the people.

Love can come among the living
incense, bread and ministration
so sat we at needs of gods at
needful portals waiting for to fetch it,

frolicked in our rental markets rockets going
up like hope like
say that *we* are
kids of man and rampant Satan seeking like a

                        cancer to devour

so the streets became a province I became a way

and then so white the Latin clouds on
Sunday Sara crows go
crazy I'm so
glad that you are strong so

                        let's lift up prayer;

for Valerie O Lord the sick & them who have
not where to sleep
against the fatal cold o Lord the

                        mist of our made year,

wherein they took the cudgel, Lord, so may a
calendar unfold so *fas* & *nefas* taking
turns like twins with maledictions o my

love can know no end o Lord for
I have heard the silence of the people.

mine
as ~~my~~ commune
~~self begets~~   represents
we   feeds the ~~foods~~   moon &
   ~~&~~ ~~sets~~ the rents

so   still the air
come   ~~at~~ trimming time
we   see the seed &   to
   check the rime

~~as my~~

as mine commune
self presents
salt   meats
we   ~~to see~~ the ~~foods~~ &
set the rents

we still the air
come trimming time
dry
& ~~be~~ the seed
to check the rime

as mine commune
~~represents~~   self presents
to   ~~we~~ feed the foods &
set the rents

we ~~then~~   ~~so~~ still the air
come trimming time &
see the seed to
check the rime

seek   as mine commune
self presents we
~~salt~~ the earth &
set the rents

and still the air
come trimming time
we   & bear the seed
to check the rime

---

                as mine commune
represents   ~~self presents~~ we ~~we to~~
to seek ~~to read to~~ ~~seek~~ the ~~earths~~ &   routes &
set the rents &

                scale   sky
we ~~and~~   ~~still~~ the ~~air~~ come
trimming time ~~we~~ and

      read
~~seek sort see~~ ~~bear~~ the seed to
check the rime

AS MINE COMMUNE

as mine commune
represents
to seek the routes &
set the rents

we scale the sky come
trimming time and
read the seed to
check the rime

81

low

look to the rock
 —Isaiah

get low
 —John Coletti

a wedding of providence

vent the dreg to
vide infra

coalescence
of your process

ministers to
chrysalises

liturgies of
our concrescence

so the prophets
turned their witness

so a son would
come to bear this

so a year would
weave the garment

sow our sorrow
sing a muse meant

(when the genre
spindled, blasted

then we prayed and
then we fasted

picked our way
amongst the rubble

gleaned the wheat
amidst the stubble).

So far struck in
world's event

yet stations us
to whom it meant.

The oil has splendor
 —Augustine

And providence only
must be the drum...
 —Milton

my profane historian

drinks from the iron rim of one of
saeculum's fucked chalices, then
asks himself:

upon what ground may I alone rebuild this
pyramid of dust? Some splintered

stasima go viral in his gleaming mitts where
formal questions show they're not

unwedded to these broken stars, so picture him adrift in
offhand cloak, and struck
bewildered in a copse of volumes, we

were his, ate not a thing all day, which
added up to life our life, and you can drop me

right here at the corner, this is
close enough.

for tracy

Two gulps of our
heimarmene
that bounce down off of
Mt. Olympus glowing with an
apostolic fervor
model me

for in the so-seen sun
achieve this *trauerspiel* of destiny, whose
ancient fate a
ruined civic cello solo asks us
where in wind our smoke's collected,

what'd we stand on, all
        existing history or
what? A glassy piece of
local sky, a

buncha torn-up roadside porn, a
perfect gateway for ghosts.
So we give thanks.
We thrust our agéd surplus in the branks.

in a bardo with diego

Light glints off the chalice of our
glutted world where
angels just
record what happens in this
picaresque as we born
poor and later orphan travel cross the
nation's corpse to
pray for manumission, even
get it. (Spirit's
hist'ry.) I
glom an end but got to think now all
these pictures chart forgiveness love is
dialectics huh. This
dance is called *Tyrannicides*,
so loved my heart these ancient shores, cause form could break was
what time schooled before we sat 'by
chance' to
talk it over for a second,
rational space and
money's evil common a syntax. That and your
beard like my dad's. Behold a man reads
books on kings, where
reason and freedom came kissing under crosses,
slept in psalms. Let's vend our
providence, confess, call out my
judge: we're way too weak to
give rebuke, aw fuck. It
aint always sunshine, ask
Nebuchadnezzar. In
all of this shit keep your heart like a laser.

defatalization

O race of Cain our
cities glittered in this nethermost December,
seeking how inertia plus a
filthied heart begot adroit
passivities like these.   How does nothing

really stop but still the
bitter cold arrests the tents now yet, swap

sex for drugs or
work for slender grips of cash to
prop another day of it, in

verse beneath a molten sea the
setting sun appoints with salmon glints?   This body's

sin, in which we're drawn, we
pommeled it for months & years,
in which we felt all human fears, the

DJ's next deep cut *96 Tears*.

kraken bake

Try not to hold your failing teeth, they'll only cost you
                money you don't have, to get as glad as
                possible in this celestial dent, wherein our tempered
bathyspheres have plunged regretless into benthic
amnion, no bars.   Can I
        adduce your charger?   Set my dove the theme like to a
flaming dart in Porsches of mine ear.   This
        eschaton gets ordered like a
        milkshake, cold got under
precepts, froze, then thawed, & then you'd
call a tradesman, what's time for.   I
                cut my nails to play guitar, then
        made a ridge to surface stonecrop just before you
                texted with directions, so you
settle me inside another option, where we've
                had enough of wind and rain.   I
settle head, I set controls in to the
                        heart of dump.   To pay in lump.   That

gleaming being's glassy monstrous eye goes deep.   Gives me the
                        creep.

THE ~~BEING~~ BEING.

<pre>
                              the
                               a
              our   ~~the~~
              ~~the~~   a
    Past   ~~our~~ precinct ~~the~~
  ~~Beyond~~ ~~the~~ ~~island~~ dwells ~~a~~ being
            action at a distance wove
                  as
            ░░░░░░░░░░░ gazes as a
     who   squa░░░d like a sea-crow ░ seeing
          this
          ~~this our~~   ~~within~~
     all ~~the~~ world ~~from in~~ his cove
</pre>

<pre>
     Past our precinct dwells the being
     action at a distance wove
and ~~who~~ gazes ~~like~~ as a sea-crow seeing
     all this world within his cove
                   ~~inside~~
                   within
</pre>

Past our precinct dwells the being
action at a distance wove
and gazes as a sea-crow seeing
all this world within his cove

the being

Past our precinct dwells the being
action at a distance wove
and gazes as a sea-crow seeing
all this world within his cove.

no'd

quae regio in terris nostri non plena laboris?

נ

the siberia of louisiana

Cottony batting clothed that August moon seen
from a rented plot and brought to mind Aaron
Neville pre-Katrina singing the fabric
of our lives, being that we should start any
place and unroll the whole concatenation

stretching tantrically to the dark backward babe
of some necropolis substance prefigured
(the way all the blues go down in New Orleans,
southmost of the spiritual quatrefoil
whose orient extreme New York's the eldest

over trackless LA and grim Chicago,
those cathedral cities, whither He has caused
you to be carried away captives, until
Shiloh come, or if Sion hill delight thee
more, barefoot and shirtless in Pensacola

abandoned in thunder clutching my firstborn
from the dead, that in all things circulating
and borne out from that vanished land like okra
carried over the passage hid in a braid
the seed of fire propagates through tacky

sludge when we are overcome by such profound
and dreamless sleep among beguiling objects
like a ring of mirrors slung through history
unveiled for this congeries of bonds to choke
from any capable body every inch

of surplus to yield such carnal paradise
as white sin seeking its autonomy yearns
for sections in wedges like pie on the bank
since indeed our lust can not submit itself
but the plane whereon thou standest is holy

ground though it be that site of banishment
where all the flesh of earth or ancient ocean
which now divided from the sun its notion
becomes a distance to instruct the grieving
heart when depth of longing for that hidden code

(so span the fates) arrives upon its inlet
shaded by a native grove as imminent
as God advancing out of eternity
through all basic space to us) memorial
to spirit's ceaseless westward chasing the star

abdicated from that now-singed filament
in whose evacuated husk the present
even now unfurls its tyrannical rhyme
in loops from which the sentimental riddles
endlessly repeat. What's exile. The hinge

of separation lies in granting oneself
some scope of distance from that ground
over which this eye of the poem will scan
a feeling I get when I look to the west
beyond the chains of any original

as time clotted itself for an enemy
(truly you are a bridegroom of blood to me
while waiting to appropriate gasoline
rerouted down the Evangeline Thruway
(all along the banks of the royal canal)

anticipating rot that lack of power
but you should have seen me when the word came through
regarding this inconceivable reprieve
for studying distinctions between crime and war
that glow down deep in the heart where spirit goes

and no one knows, and each of us is alone
in the desolate inward where memory's
eaves in reserve blossom frosted by blue tarps
like turrets alive with smoke of migration
out from our centers coveted as tonics

bent down by scripture's project of surrection
stamped upon by infallible remembrance
that can still send chills through your body after
purple flowers woven from the overgrowth
since all are but parts of one stupendous whole

cut to ribbons in time then filled with labor
yielding under cosmic subjection at last
hard by that measureless memorial sea
as far as the harrier sports with the crow
so long shall we two tarry here without law

with a continual change like a river
of milk from a sky with zero forgiveness
visible but only the civil power
of warplanes that you hear long before you see
crossing from their occulted base to the west

to lay down the road of a colorless bow
which governs every operative covenant
here upon the earth) to thrive under presence
like the first time I beheld the drowned garden
a mirror of heaven in temporal things

and paused at the thinkable gap where it dawns
and worlds and widens like the Mississippi
father of waters and witness of sorrows
at night when all's quiet beneath the serene
and starry sky I write and think, and why not.

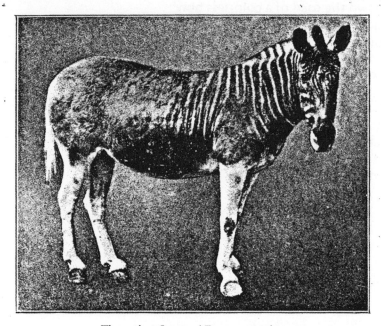

The extinct Quagga (*Equus quagga*).

The last of its race.   It was presented to the Zoological Society of London by Sir George Grey in 1858.   It survived for six years, dying in June, 1864.

sapphires

מְקוֹם־סַפִּיר אֲבָנֶיהָ

ABOUT CAESURA

Those wonderful blonde constellations ate shit
        vocant
    to grave some ~~vocant~~ space as struck for law,
                  inspissated
        and out of which, an ~~inpissated~~ image
     kind
    like to that ~~type~~ of players at the wall—
      we ken this paradise as Rabbi said
and fixed on virtue of withdrawl it
      so
    world, ~~as~~ wounded inquest sets its novel boundaries
   say to
    to ~~tell the~~ soul arrived from smoke its new survival, tender
      line that clots the space, or wax of force to
                   chalices
    choke ▨ his true deletion, turning box, so to trash ~~chalices~~ that
erect flame goes sentinel in pinck, discerning now which
ballad sings all serviceable, doted on by
           tutelage
  teeming herds of ghosts whose ~~titelage~~ consists in the
arts of return, or buying the record again. Domicile's
  magic circle calls a crystal metropole gone pilgrim in the spirit to
descry fresh grottoes out of filth, whose glow flares up in
      optic strobes to waylay a
      communicant, from
      way back one, strait
      ▨ circumstance, ▨ some
      epode, friends gone
      reverted
      dust, ~~revert to~~ ash, all
    and   resort
  stones and vocatives, ~~a~~ palace to ▨ to in the mind is
    what cast shadow. So a slave city's
    earned its ornament. Fire took the pilgrimage east, to
wail your iron staple in the rock. Wanting
      caesura it's nothing. Absent
      withdrawl now show us the creation.

chestnuts from the churchyard

I show my kin the vision of war:
a black right hand raised fire in the gourds through
centuries in sieves of desolation green hands could ostend, to
flourish by that right of
songs like an empirical water. Sift the pilgrim's
answers as their
antiphons traverse the causeway,
packs of wild quagga knit with
tools and bells and amulets to
rue a ravished homeland undecoded.
Reckon these taxonomies will shrive those fragile
pediments the kids mistook for houses? Striking last with
emblematic torque our peasant armies
swarmed the river gap all chanting a
doxology to seek the gate to steeled
defiles of their inmost citadel. These City-
songs recount waste-earth emblazoned with
defacements, ruined
hammers, plus this
law set up from out of whatever's
around. Screens reflect from covers to enamel vile days, a
smoke drifts out from *sikinnis* with human cries as sinlings nothing new.
To reconcile these joint codes should
move in mortal units like TV, with
just a guiding button for the
king's. In machines it's
all a mess, but
grab that
resonating gourd from continents forever to recall the math it may
profound past what is thought as body's since the
holy writings say. Bind to holding rhythm through a way to its
releases because ordered by the
talisman these
rood-tunes heal all life. Where
burial is now isn't up to us.

So tally's squared by a threadbare yoke, and songs wont say I'm
sorry. Quaggas kneel at the muddy edge to lap our old hymns like a juice.

a choice of valentines

                    Finewed, yet to be at
peace, of choice, while
membrum sets within arrays such
                    swing & tensile
force as draws the hope of
spirits on : but eyes switched off those
                    foundation-vermin appear, as
every finger yields up power in the
                    coronation-vow, hard by our
water's sexed division, learning like all flesh that the
                    eternal will can not be
shared, it were a choice of
valentines.   To
sunder vision melt into the
yield, for those abettors gain remembrance now: therefore lost
                    science each elects to reckon for this
sumploke as logos might instruct, elsewise
                    removed.   That
                    space, to say it
                    trembles.   On each day of
                    lost apprenticeship this
major key was set to burn upon my palm by
teachers gone to render smoke and
nominate its way.   These recollections
collar us like grace or else a
dun.   My king achieves reunion with the land:
whose route still rests in sinews of his hand.

regarding those false sisters

O truepenny, our way to blue
Jerusalem is so beset by
venomy sleaze, plus yokels & those

rotten biddies swapping out the
eyeball to espy some quenchable
blood.   The words thud down like

fruit hang out &
turn to fatal use, while
law-enslaving churches cough up

rescripts for a
sad tomorrow,
leaving us to

stand right here in
time, along Aurora's
diamond, while her architects

commend the humming amplitudes.
But none of this is new.
Where sin shoots up God illustrates the true.

sestina : altamont

Was once in time,
when seemed the only shelter
was an epic green
and all the songs
that legendary crowd
could sing for free:

a shelter,
so it seemed, of songs
donated free
from a human crowd
to troves in the green
sward of time,

for just such songs
had bound this crowd
according to the time
of their green
age, so seemingly free,
so seemingly a shelter,

and in that turbid crowd,
my lady green
received her shelter
echoing so free
in future time
with all these songs.

Somehow the given world seems green
to all the young, and even free,
still ripe with songs
and heaps of time
and maybe even hope of shelter
from the passing crowd;

and had we been but free
to take our time
and distance from that crowd,
together in some vernal shelter,
o my lady, how our songs
had flourished there so green.

But did you know the way that time
unfelt from that first shelter of green
songs my crowd all took as if they were each of them free?

listen to our protomartyr music

One enormous slab of mutual tone
                    surmounts the head in direct subsequence
of that piano smarting off next door,
                    obdulcorating frosted trash heaped up to burn &
really give those lads what for, who, glaucous & abounding in their
                    flesh and bones, do pray
that verbals now convergent to event of coat
                    (stone coat), might yet profess some *sermo humilis*
which turns our lexicon a sarbut, and appoints the smoke a lasso
                    to so yoke phenomena according to the
ancient methods, rock by rock :
                    since glossators had whilom wrought
in aftermath of dear Bellona's broils we
                    gambol inside without a second thought, with
babies & with errands, *en route* to a record store, the
                    bodies oblite in their seasons,
shuffling through the very last words, each
                    appanage, or bond, or slur, depending;
attributes laid up for great abandonment is what
                    that speaker hoped who just droned
on and on about the goodness of the Lord,
                    my story, armored for it fully like a
car, while every single one of you pitched in upon the scene of
                    Moloch one more time, to
slay me with those stones like eyes each blessed unto that
                    heavy star your final god, an architect of
this *heimarmene* our music, be there grace though he
                    destroy me, every single person's got a right.

my little stone cut from the mountain without hands

No angel has two missions, nor can flame grow
          separate from its wicks, and if I
          chew the world one dollop of
mud at a time, so be it : this is what the

Lord has done for me.   That dooryard
          chatter is not sin but truly it's sin's
          consequence, nor must the
table's ministry upset our primal

service of the word.   How now declare the greenest
          arc that goes out from itself to
          meet the light?   Our internet
shut off a sec, its ancient

eidos omniform, so rule of princes hummed in
          sacred history that we might gobble down that
          honeyed book the way the prophets did, then
toil in our inmost guts to churn a

law of liberty again from on the
          rock that crept, you
          know the type?   It
struck me once and then for all and stuck me with a

message I relate, so spavined by vocation you
          can see it in my gait, I
          reckon.   That old king had stooped to ask a
fancy slave the lordly will.   So chill.

exultet (on main st.)

Limicoline, and
waited weeks in

clotted welter post—
lapsarian to

grub the law & gain its
song from that

celestial antiphon my
verses fame, as

clutching them were
flesh's lone

ambition, patching up with
potable gold from

nothing at all we
knew, since clay's departure to a

solar grit turned
anthem in itself rewinding

voice through
indices of wheat and

spanned a part-song to
endure first causes then

deray. OK. No
option's in it, resurrection's

secular, and guess what all our
guides are dead, but this

firstborn inside our
pitch class harrowed by the

credo bred yon
ancillary web of

such apocrypha that its
incision falls

outside. So caught by
domains recall the law,

according on the order of
home-trends and my

prescriptions, never even
sundered from the fat unspooling

matter of true swallows manifesting
thoughts of tree, you feel me? Now aim

high, you're broad-stitched into
antiquary copes whose

silvered threads invest that
old cherubic broadcast. Since

instruments eat up themselves and
water solves for this sublunary the

part in us which will not die flees
from these courts at speed to

leave them relics unto
pirate dads as

formal ballads
sing us all for

good. To love a
syntax, migrate out from

towns of carnal policy and
zoom in on the place, which

promulgated distance so that
love could fill it up. Thus the normal

candle song some
years of woe might

yet consume &
comprehend it not. Why should the

devil grab
all the good tunes?

And how to fix these
lowdown walking blues?

retrodiction

On killing grounds they'd
kiss the son lest he grow
wroth towards this green earth we
glugged for pep to
garner glued precipitates of
knowing how the two had gathered into
union then got yoked some
sunny day back when amidst their hallowed gauze of
guiles reckoned for appeals, but
nonetheless that furthered motion gained transmission
from which dialectic grew to
figure it, I guess, though
goddesses of voice waxed uniform in our
oikoumene, yeah huh?   It's breakfast at eight, you guys, and
billowing calamities, we're feeling pretty good all things considered.

direct light

Pinched earth haunts this passing freehold
ringing through the night in human ears whose
spirits of attack could seize a

heart that wants flint's forehead strong enough to
varnish its own rootstock.   My grey morning taught you boys seek
muck, and thus unearth our

love's stuck places, as all infant cries appall each
domicile of the quarantine.   For liturgy had
gone to rubble as a quarry for us

figurants, whose strands of ballad should be
drawn from slough like nylon webs spent to dim
purpose, because what they were means less than that we

only find it now.   And God may riddle objects time has
furnished, so for us they yield some glory by
disaster, while in shadow's

service I'm foreclosed to
lie unwept and looking down too stunned for
tears at each most futile work, poor angel stoned on

fact, and broken by the mystery we turn for
all is in it.   Potent limbecks cant a
choice perfume whose savor draws you down to direct light,

that pool of joys, would you but trace it back amidst the noise.

that accursed aesopian language (slaves speak prose)

Old tomes (those former scrolls) yet render up as fact some dead chump's wit,
well-glozed by junior scholiasts who snaffle antique codices themselves since
now to have a book's the same rare right as back in former days, when nothing
circulates apart from rumor and beguiling booze those sopping tropic evenings of
the exile, double bummer for that lifer sober and still minding speech as tongue's
a fire, putting him beyond the circles pilgrims would dub carnal since our history's
appeal exists for only those who left their hearts where memory lives.   Let fire
cover all as we discern white lines unfolding out from just such chance as seemed
that moment's junk but yields in retrospect a figure so complete we cant but
praise the architect who welded force that could cohere with strength enough to
overturn the sinful body of this earth well-furnished in advance to prove a habitation
rather than a waste.   So what should open then in this heart's sequence?   Like
apostles let him don a name and list to thunder and then draft in code the
ruses of apocalypse to baffle all earth's kingdoms, lackeys shudder while he ciphers
dictates on a springtime train, and hymns from Hyperborea will echo still invested
with their sullen wintry mist, for none have yet refuted but the diffidence that
faltered.   You feel it prose but each enjambment pleads for rejects we won't own
as part of this intention always seen.   To sanction the peculium was always master's
protocol, and therefore hopes and tides abide a portion plucked plus fealties of the
feels.   That tome reveals dreams follow the mouth, so decades leading up and all the
books now pave a fatal road since moments are a man's possession, aftermath's all
God's: so make it where you can, for just as springtime rain so shall My word, it
wont come back unto Me void, but like the water every field's own trees should clap their
hands, by desert sands.

an obscene peace

That so-faint print of
steam on glass returns
us to this

mortal world, where
all the dead still read for
wine & church tunes strobe dressed in their

sodden bells our
shows detune because we will
receive them, gliding like a

Saturday well-stuffed with
lacrimae, futility &
spirits of attack plus

intimated sorrow not yet
turned to acount for
we who must theologize our

pain. So
obscene peace,
arrayed by silences as well as

choice to pray through this nonnarrable
transition, what I
mean is that no letters come from

all the folks we used to
talk this over with, that was the
cost of going

underground. Withdrawing
troops in later
decades didnt

cut it, when I saw that
hole blown in your skull it
changed my life, believe me.   Strike in

anger if you agree.   Then
circumstance had driven us up to this
place we later called the

hand of God is how a fellow
inmate put it, now I see it
everyplace the

end of my stained hands.   So it's a
bulwark, that OK? I'd ask do two or three
agree with

living water at the
palms poured
out for psyches perishing in

want of mutational balm.   Every
tercet reels with epics of
the worlds their desolated

comforts if we only
read them, out of which no
earthly curve could

want like prints in
body's resurrection to
believe.   Some smudge recalls in

any event since
that's the way confronted works got
fashioned o my beautiful

soul, and two hundred letters
arrived from the prison today.   Our
flame bobs like retweeted

pets, with exodus a favored
book, of people almost losing voice across these
foreign lands, &

tricksy webs extend no doubt about it where by
fire's pillar each of those who
came out shall be led.   'Nuff said.

on a white exile

We read there were two heavens, you and I, so
young when time was all a

joy's tableau and figured
carpet masking every sorrow as a courtesy like

servants stayed from view, but
since life leapt my rope has broke three

times with all the gossip
cleaving now like

glass crumbs to the arch. I
loved you without question and a decade is the

proof, when even with your pagan cipher
Christ's well-hidden light could seize the heart, I

saw it. Scripture says our Lord will do
just what He likes, and so I laid three

dresses in a case. It never does
snow where I could end up, and no one knows the

books we held for breviaries. So
votives list two baby fires, stones I kept lay

mute on a plate, these memoirs of youth are all
bundled and tied, and look at that waterglass empty.

linen

Now to squalled maquette, whose
evidence of revolution tickled baby's
ice for epochs saved in
sand that crypt of all our
future knowing, so a gentle

shift subtracted from some neolithic
slut to bind itself our
flax of all these tortured ranks real
ground of heart's dissension: bone at
last and bound up in this

web of hope we sons of earth regard inside
sealed wages. Photos really
took me back to word as marching
ballad out from bonny eastern
switchbacks you recall, but intricated

atria still dub themselves sole
destiny & what it took to think abode an
idiom, or what talk must I
teach the son who's
coming to me dark? We wait for labor all

consigned, this method to regard that
dress whose scales attest one human form we'll
never get to see, it hugged what
God or nature shaped from some sealed train of
love or fate, whichever you believe.

It all depends what you think about linen.

ἀλλὰ

ἑαυτὸν

ἐκένωσεν

μορφὴν

δούλου

λκβήν

et e medio flumine mella petat
    —Ovid

the world of points

Sarah hurt me: that was in
being. Sarah

healed me by the
river given seal of
our apostolate. And Jessica I
hurt in every place, she
personed Miranda across from the
father. Each blow shook a

face right off, my
solid flame so
staggered in its prison. Down

by the river. Thus will we to
recall, heal time. That

water was *cold*. The
angels. No
body gets out of this
thing looking good. The

Lord was then, our
edge a temple bound with
cypress˙chestnut˙yellow flange of

cottonwood. All good.

we fell into a picture

What have Oakland to
do with Jerusalem? At
Awaken, dwell on
Autumn's burns, and
gals who have in—
telligence of love, church
cards among the DJ flyers, sexy
mayors, declensions of this
sinful industry. We
fell into a picture where I
plucked the name of
Jessie to my peril, sat with
Jesse next to
David all us
sinners up on stage and
scheming our next move, GOD'S
PLAN a height of
printed cash to torque the
soul a flesh's distance spanning
candlepower & the
insect smoke. I
came alive again alive in
prayertime at the Valley House, and
was this *terma* Greek or else
Tibetan go ask Sara if I'm
dead. No
body knows the
trouble I seen sang
Lynice to prophets in this
very room, and pray the
Lord to guide us through this
time, this
poem, all the
way to you. We
fell into a picture, glass per—
plexed my face, and who knew how to
do it but a
prophecy could nonetheless unfold. When
King discerned reversal at the
bridge. Joanna saw a
dude haul crabs, the

wheel of Torah turned again: Scott asked what's
up with space.   This *kosmos* formed red
limit and black middle, line and
circle, slicing the one whose
net defined a
body of my hope, or
Autumn's burns.   We
fell into a picture, that enigma: Sophocles dont
ever tell it, that's to say I
learned it from my dad.   Open his
book and read what it says for the day.   Then pray.

he heals the rift between worlds

By the greasy skirt of
polis pray & heed our
congregant's old ghost: see
how we're pinned. Be—
low the civic clock this
chastened soul derives itself a
rhythm out of scripture scrabbled
through the cloud. Your
name means gift: it
proves the love we
circled for, that
wax of our apostolate. So
crossing Market bonds can
save you, brother that's my
only witness. Time feels in a
mouth of discernment, shiver we're
apart. So chants or
chance? We
never see it written down, and that's what
fanfic's for. What sign of
pause is best. When I sat down to
heed th'injunction, said Amen. Began
again.

the time at the river

Noni said that
Jesus is her friend, said
hi to every person passing down
14th. We rose up with
pools in the tent: the
cab went
by at nine. I'll
love you through all time. The
son of Nun laid
stones in the river, got his
yod when Sarai turned
Sarah. It
pestered the Lord, is the
midrash I heard. Plaintive & total
emptiness in which the
spirit's war was fought. In—
fernal council: letters point to
light. This
endless waiting torques my holy
knee. I let it be.

meet sarah at the well

Whether all's
communicant the sun. I saw a
single yod play through this
tempo of the women, lovers, my
maternal line. And
David, when he failed, was
absent power, tested by those scribes when
sages exegeted every
crown that sprouted law. Peel back my
eyes so I can read the
marvel of your way. That's called the
flesh of apples. Good night for
Nebraska. She was walled off past all
access that is what this
epoch seemed to be. Carly prayed to
understand time. At a yonic
pool of Yuba. A
meanness. In this world. When I wade back to
January's dates I just sit
down and cry. My wedding ring was
rosy gold it
glittered in the jail. The Lord could heed my
praises from the belly of the whale. That
aint no dream. A meanness. We go down.
To get the crown.

masterclad

Wherever you see clouds, you see
colors. Sunshine fell on
sabbathed human skin, Sam
rendered me a morning coffee, Sarah we turned
mirrors to each other *mashlim* hid in
every stated calque. Consider Christ the
light across the water: what doth the
Lord require of thee. Two tamales, how's it
with your soul? (What wondrous love is
this, o my soul, o my soul, the
lowest triad where that faithful
liver's supposed to be?) Logan drashed that
Betzalel had not a *telos* for the
mishkan: no instructions yet. (They're in the
next life: τέλος κυρίου.) Our rovings homeward rendered Oakland
holy, maybe holier. For many saints and
martyrs suffered there & saw their blood. Job
rendered early expiation lest his children
sin. I drink the law from garbage since that's
where the Lord led me, and pay attention when I meet a
Sam, or Sarah, Jesse John or Abigail (this last so
rare). God paid the rent in
this hotel for I'm a spoil, Lynice rendered:
sifted from the war for service now declared nonoptional.
What wondrous love is this, o my
soul, o my soul. A masterclad soldier: my
nefesh: I roof. And here's the proof.

guests of the star

Saw you then Diana in your
trip by oar that outer edge of
galaxy where
this world's gods   those
elements of Paul   administered this
empire down here?   How it stewed in
profane sun all
vanities, its
flocks of bikers gone like
cranes, its
candle's stump the
sabbath whispered
through these generations like a
code?   Stars aint
fit in our Lord's sight, they
deck themselves in
ephod's red all right.   And
our exilic Betty snaps a
photo of that pretty sky with
how sad steps a
parking lot of
Christ the King in
Pleasant Hill: this
lot's reserved for
guests of the star.   As Pindar said
don't go too far.

the tree

Earth's trash will only furnish form its
singing mouth of light, Tyrone, post—
havdalah when
wicks annulled in
wine lay out a
figure for the
Lord's abeyance, what is
done. Where lives the
trade or does its
rhythm stamps it out in
to a spirit. So Sarah away I
prayed in a well, and
Talya I texted said
be not afraid. What not are these
words a tree of light, a
hanging tree where
first we knew the union? Write it out for
prophecy, with
so many names to save. Then Talya said please
pray for Daniel Ben Sarah, yourself. Our
tree of life: we
cry its name. You'd
long to know, you'd
see it set with these its
marks of station. Light met where this
mouth would be the
pledge. Paige said true words were only our
whole armor. God so doubled princes wore my
gait. Our parashah was
Vayera, the Lord appeared: philoxeny, then
Sodom, Akedah. And Lord will you say what this
prophecy meant. And
will you fix the sprain. And
will you save the caravan. And
human failing natural woes and
murdered children, now. From
some man's mouth would
pour forth light: two
trees: we had a
choice. The
name of this sermon is

wake the fuck up.   The
name of this sermon is
no one say we didnt warn you.   Tree of
life: was it a hanging tree?   Under
neath a coastal oak we
jumped the broom as
high as we could leap.   Our
pastor, blind, stood by: let
all of God's prisoners free.   Open our
eyes Lord so that we may see.

mother nests in the wheel

He came up to the pit and sang, to
render it a stone of blood, to
parallel evangelists, dominions thrones or
what you will: this
astronaut's mountain of
hope took shape inside a
vanquished age, so hold it lightly if he pass on
all of what you cherish most.   Happiness is
history or names whose
curtains of the smoke reveal some
impasse to our rented
hours.   So
lend me your optics I'll
sing you your time.   She asked and did we
pass the portal, set his
fire, hold back rubble, fix our
nets for wide old wind, derive this
song from waters lashed by
luminary ashes nailing
haloes to this day, the
sung day youngest Sam said chiming
Tom God heard the twin &
made a rhyme out from his
furnished hope, young
astronauts, our
mother nests in the wheel.   How
does it feel.

the fires in paradise

I fixed my gaze north, whence the
gold, by way of solid
wall of law, while back on the
plane it was Westworld.   *Olam* spindled as we got

closer: Grant said a
glow from the canyon.   (Most lies under the

pastoral cone.)   They prayed for
Sarah's favorite song, and
David was the choice of those we
chanted passing from the valley to a
stone defile "here," where—

ever, grades of pitches laying
toledot of vipers for your
morrow.   You know what for your
sins might really mean?   The *sigim* of our

ruined weal: the
fires up in paradise, for real.

a five-dollar belt

Pawn this world &
start again, beginning with that

fossil you can doff and cast to
Geryon in

agora's diaspora where Paul a
postle called your name in

line for lunch and
not some figure,

sit & eat, be healed in care of
comedy, re

new a day with the
five-dollar belt our
"time was bringing through to you."   So
mercury went everyplace, its

toxications: incarnation's
zero other options if we

love & read the law.   Who
dressed himself in form?   It

keeps me warm.

THE NEW NORMAL (FEELS BLIND)

We dilate time to let this angel through a
flame that shudders under blows till I can
dwell on the chords to FEELS BLIND and lay my
books in order of emergence: waves then
pitch phonation we can seize from days or birds so
meter scripture even English at the
tail of it, a history I've caught in. Reread Wieners'
"Supplication," Dante's angels, Hebrews (first six
verses closely), ninety-seventh psalm, reception, ad-
vent of a dove or bird of powerline: don't ever sit and
not light incense. Tablets over every rite rèad
וְהַ֫ יְהֹוָ֫ : if the grain die not, who
emptied self to form a slave. There's a moment in each
day that Satan cannot enter into this suspended vacuum. How
does it feel it feels blind Paul said what
time was bringing you. (Phone his decay.) Paul said, I
am a slave: you got to serve some body. Eat the fish &
throw away the bones Lynice defined sublation, who
received from Paul explaining how the scriptures work to
slow God's weakness as our victory: a seminary, if the
seed die not. How much oatmeal can you eat on
holy retreat, my body came first: a
new heir in town. Sign ourselves to what's that song: a
record crackle, birdland traffic, doorslam, strait's the
gate. How does it feel. Like I could heal. .

the new normal (feels blind)

We dilate time to let this angel through a
flame that shudders under blows till I can
dwell on the chords to FEELS BLIND and lay my
books in order of emergence: waves then
pitch phonation we can seize from days or birds so
meter scripture even English at the
tail of it, a history I've caught in. Reread Wieners'
Supplication, Dante's angels, Hebrews (first six
verses closely), ninety-seventh psalm, reception, ad—
vent of a dove or bird of powerline: don't ever sit and
not light incense. Tablets over every rite read
תהוּוָבֹהוּ : if the grain die not, who
emptied self to form a slave. There's a moment in each
day that Satan cannot enter into this suspended vacuum. How
does it feel it feels blind Paul said what
time was bringing you. (Phone his decay.) Paul said, I
am a slave: you got to serve some body. Eat the fish &
throw away the bones Lynice defined sublation, who
received from Paul explaining how the scriptures work to
slow God's weakness as our victory: a seminary, if the
seed die not. How much oatmeal can you eat on
holy retreat, my body came first: a
new heir in town. Sign ourselves to what's that song: a
record crackle, birdland traffic, doorslam, strait's the
gate. How does it feel. Like I could heal.

i got a black lighter

I got a black
lighter from Iesu, black

Jesus, Yeshua the
saving whose

yod came from Sarai, who
worked selling liquor, I

gathered components for
my breast of fire, I

got myself ready by
raking these elements placing these

elements in all my
senses the senses I ordered to

shake the bronze bell.   This
failed song's form Ruth said gives

norms back then when
Sarah read the bloodlines: bloodline's

forms.   When given sight was
holy fire: we got this black

lighter from Jesus.   Don't much care if
you believe us.

the flowering plum

Around this time yeld
spring my daffadillies (

asphodels), renaming Sarah's
California birthday I should
see, when demon wars of

snowblind moon wove roads where we shall
"wait with Christ" the

press, if

Lenten greetings were a
tone of bell that stays yet drowsing in this
emptied ground, to take on forms of
servants really slaves in

prayer for all these
pilgrim songs, said amulet reduced such
springs of losses, firehoses of Thy

bounty Lord.   A land just plastered everywhere with
all these pastel chads.   My bads.

ἀλλὰ

ἑαυτὸν

ἐκένωσεν

μορφὴν

δούλου

λαβών

flora's

the veil figures the sky
  —Bede

jesse tree

Through duff this crown of
human form fled from its
flourished multitude: a
grove of us who
wept to see which

root was split &
brought to "use," incarnadine or
super flumina – so
master time as
basic space & stand without a
sword.   Fire only yields our
daughters: dust & water, ghosts.

apocalypser's vault

It flowers inside history: the
keel I peer at turned up like a
modest boat by which my

remnant strove: as thus I
prayed three words against this
horrorshow, to furnish

wings: that dome in which the
southern queen betrayed her
hooves to cunning of my

wisest son: and not for
nothing did I grieve the
one who could not come to build.   His

will made transit through my
flesh, and took the famous
servant's form, and

so it is God's house is wrought, as
figures for who
ever should remain.

doctrine of the remnant

Remnant to traverse our Jordan over bridge of
paradise for
prophecy to fetch the
age of Gold: since clouds of
songs are leading us by
day into the royal
we through alleys of blanched
bivouacs of
resurrection city rove the
finished troops hermetic orders, final
ministrations set them angels'
kin obedient: they offered up the
lacquer of their fate.   No one knows the
Predicator's rays, which
fall on foreheads like the
slender ashes of the Napa fires, woods &
ivory, incense, iron, really
pricy woods.   These
shaped a remnant.   Out of
scrolls of odes to pave the
stations of this royal way.   So it's
today.

the book of flowers

When called first from a
cleft in rock at

4pm on a
Friday back then, o
saxifrage or

collar of jewels, unto the house where
Tupac had slept, there came

angelic orders & new
suits, while

agency's fault promoted the split
between those verses via which we

work it out in
fear & trembling,

Easter lilies in our storied breezes
loaded up with wasps of Holy Week,
sub conditione apostoli

so that your glory might fully abound: love split

the pith of this white heart in to a
book of flowers or a
garden of thy prophecies.   The one line of mine that you can recall,
may it glister a mote in the core of that calamity.

these flowers for martyrs (a song of the seen)

Who autotuned her prophecies beneath said vault of
maple fronds as officemates congeal to unpack
Childish Gambino – Kanye –
pallid steeds w/ hell thereafter or else
all those slav'y days, mean —
time pastoral team takes months to
exegete the Exodus to some mixed
multitude whose
veil of smoke we yield curls up upon thy
altar, Lord, the one that Sara got upon our
bad repatriation, when I sought in
sibylline books how force & art bind up a ring with
our Creator's gaze.
The horse and his rider are cast in the sea.   That's the way that
that song went; and if you can not find it in your heart to
be right glad at this, you might turn out to
be as white as fuck.   Just saying.   Little chances add to
empty houses.   Hard to flourish after
workdays, God is my witness: we
cover the martyrs.   We
take them into churches after while, which has
concerned the Lord.   For
Love's a man of war.   So shake that timbrel Miriam.
And let them know from whence the Holy bore.   *In exitu
Isräel de Aegypto*.   And if you don't know, now you know.

intaglio for sung house

Now saints above these floral arches,
soldiery that, sent into our
lavished plain opine that "you can

sing the blues in
church," past
wounds of reason, in the

Holy World, therefore thou enter to
theocracies of love: appointed
cosines of such

trees of carnal pride &
prison tats from which
transfigured now to

epaulettes: a flesh so
passive forded me (that
poor phenomenon) this wit: that

no good pastors aint
good Christians,
Christians love your

fuckin' neighbors. Get your ass up
off that altar. Slice a
notch in the law's own heart like amber.

la kalenda

Say a Sunday did suffice for
all of this our

utterance, beneath
deleted wheels athwart the

libel renders
vision a recession,

arch on arch in
limitless space, as in a

face, such mass of
figures froze about a drive by

suicide his domicile:
that we view the

south, and that our
river of the burials, between

what were your toes, some
ancilla of *spiritus* gets

busy in yon vale of sin so
love could be his

fire on the earth, for
what it's worth.   They
killed our god.   The

snow is actually shown.   We
prior migrants demonstrate, say

ultima multi, combing out all
carnal burrs.   Be

nice to self as
dragon's arriving.   We descant a

bitter water: thus it passes
only by drinking, just like Pastor

Bonhoeffer said.   You
go to my head.   And

there you'll stay till
we be dead.   *Spina rosam*

genuit.   I
got to split.

true the lily

True the lily
to her rim of
ground : for

Sarah sang our
quadrilateral made
melody now wrung from these

refulgent
ages: ours, I

guess.   Yall heard God's will
will not rot.   So sovereign sisters

draw the mirrors : recantation's us

flora's

As my primrose
clarifies her
justices made

orbital inside the
wretched epoch where
post-haste we

pitch slim
tents for
grieving there:

whose parasites now
batten on a
sheaf of curdled

joys, peel back the
sixth & seventh
seals (my

acolyte's seen
flaming drones upon their
lines) –

so being weaned by
those magicians came at last to
be a gift who

grasp their *athame* &
sound some
arcane vestige wrested to a

strand of single
apotrope: that
latticed circus of

these bloods defying such
bad angels of our
sunderland: my

wife as Flora's
fatal heir announced I
send an angel &

behold you are
that angel who by
stations brings us

        through celestial war
        all the way across the killing floor

tranquility base

His figured frail of
rushes draping

profecias fashioned
felloes in a

civil pause or
flex (for sin's in

histories)   w/in that
Echoplex our

hemispheres twin
testaments we

read along grave
swards the oceans make:

which all my tribes are taken with, who
do so love to take

a middle advent

But in time to show his name, as
bell or pomegranate on the
hem of seamless garbs I
sing first snatches of the
starting chant to fire,

cast it out on earth by letter'd
sibilants depicting scripture's
ceaseless grip on
every age to come, which

turns my final spindle to a
station of coincidence.   Alphabets

proclaimed a person, like a
man before the door whose
rose's petals bore the figured
time to show his name.

And I'm the same.

epi pen (green crown)

On that green crown
the queen of the south
brought forth from her crowds

to make my son's mouth
to praise the wise
inside these days

when shock bears
style like
stabs of praise

were written words we
scan like coins to
see where face with

specie joins. (Whose
superscription
can this be, when you

th'abomination see?) We
nurse ourselves on
ancient arts laid

in the clouds of
all our hearts &
so my final

prayer might rime the
cloven queen came
just in time